THE SECRET LIFE OF A
TIGER

Text copyright © 2013 Przemysław Wechterowicz
Illustrations copyright © 2013 Emilia Dziubak
Translated by Antonia Lloyd-Jones

First published in the English language in 2017 by
words & pictures, Part of The Quarto Group
6 Orchard, Lake Forest, CA 92630

A CIP record for the book is available from the Library of Congress.

British Library Cataloguing in Publication Data available on request

ISBN: 978-1-68297-154-3

1 3 5 7 9 8 6 4 2

Printed in China

Przemysław Wechterowicz   Emilia Dziubak

THE SECRET LIFE OF A
TIGER

words & pictures

Hey! Look who we've spotted.
He's big and stripy, with a mouth full of
sharp, white teeth. Do you know who he is?
Yes, that's right, he's a ...

TIGER.

He's still sound asleep. But soon, when a ray of light
tickles his face, he'll lazily raise his right eyelid,
then his left, and then ...

"**Aaaaagrrrrrrrhhhhh ...**
well, that was a good sleep. Hello, my name
is Tiger and I live in the jungle. I'm brave and
cheerful, and I'm really looking forward
to spending some time with you."

"I lead a pretty regular life.
During the day I wander about the
neighborhood, chat with my friends,
do some thinking, take a nap,
listen to the sounds of the jungle, and
sometimes I have a bite to eat."

"Talking of which, would you believe it? Apparently there are stories going around the jungle ..."

"Now, really, do I look like someone who would bite?!?"

"It's a lie! I've never bitten anyone in my life!"

"Well, OK, maybe sometimes! But I always try to swallow my guests whole. And I swear by my father's tail that I do it with love!"

"The truth is, there's more to me than meets the eye.
In the evening, when the sleepy Sun leaves the sky
and the gentle Moon rises, I leap into action.
Because at this time my secret life begins ..."

"First, I creep up on a little baby elephant ... "

"... and chop up a delicious fruit salad for him!"

"Next, I sneak up to a group of orangutans ..."

"... to give them the hairstyle
of their dreams!"

"I pounce on eggs that have fallen
from a parrot's nest ..."

"... and hatch them myself!"

"I hypnotize busy ants with
my stare and with one flick of my tail..."

"... build them a magnificent new
anthill!"

"I leap in among the snoozing tapirs ..."

"... and we have a cheerful dance!"

"And when I spot a dozing cobra, hanging
from a tree, with a single swipe of my paw ..."

"... I gently lay the beautiful
creature on a bed of leaves."

"Roaaar!

So now you know what I really
enjoy doing, I hope you won't
think too badly of me."

"Maybe he's
not so bad
after all."

"Can you hear that?

It's the sound of the dawn tickling

the sleepy Sun awake.

Time for me to find a little hideaway

and get some rest."

"Goodbye! And don't forget—you can't believe all the stories you hear in the jungle.

A tiger's secret life is often more wonderful than you think."